HARPER

An Imprint of HarperCollinsPublishers

Written by Alexander Cox and Craig Jelley
Edited by Craig Jelley
Designed by Joe Bolder, John Stuckey, Sam Ross and Andrea Philpots
Illustrations by Ryan Marsh, John Stuckey, and Joe Bolder
Special thanks to the entire Roblox team

Shutterstock.com image credits: khuruzero, Just2shutter, ArtSimulacra, robtek, Zakharchuk

All stats featured in this book were based on information publicly available on the Roblox
platform and were correct as of March 2018

ISBN 978-0-06-286260-0

18 19 20 21 22 RTLO 10 9 8 7 6 5 4 3 2 1

First US Edition, 2018

Spending time online is great fun! Here are a few simple rules to help younger fans stay safe
and keep the internet a great place to spend time. For more advice and guidance, please see
page 70 of this book, or go to www.connectsafely.org/Roblox

- Never give out your real name – don't use it as your username.
- Never give out any of your personal details.
- Never tell anybody which school you go to or how old you are.
- Never tell anybody your password except a parent or guardian.
- Be aware that you must be 13 or over to create an account on many sites. Always check
the site policy and ask a parent or guardian for permission before registering.
- Always tell a parent or guardian if something is worrying you.

Stay safe online. Any website addresses listed in this book are correct at the time of going to
print. However, HarperCollins is not responsible for content hosted by third parties. Please be
aware that online content can be subject to change and websites can contain content that is
unsuitable for children. We advise that all children are supervised when using the internet.

INSIDE THE WORLD OF
ROBLOX

CONTENTS

MEET SOME OF THE ROBLOX FAMILY 8-9

ROBLOX RETROSPECTIVE 10-11

ANOTHER BREAKOUT YEAR! 12-13

FIRST DAY IN ROBLOX 14-15

TOP 10 MOST-PLAYED GAMES ON ROBLOX 16-17

PIXELATEDCANDY'S FAVORITE GAMES! 18-19

AVATAR EVOLUTION 20-21

DEVELOPER LESSONS: GAME DESIGN 22-23

PLATFORMER 24-25

GAMES YOU MAY HAVE MISSED 26-27

RICKYTHEFISHY'S FAVORITE GAMES! 28-29

ROBLOX GALLERY OF IMAGINATION 30-31

HOTTEST ROBLOX TRENDS 32-33

TOP 10 MOST-PLAYED GAMES ON ROBLOX 34-35

ROBLOX CALENDAR 36-37

5TH ANNUAL BLOXY AWARDS HIGHLIGHTS 38-39

GAMES YOU MAY HAVE MISSED 40-41

INSIDE ROBLOX HQ 42-43

TOP 10 MOST-PLAYED GAMES ON ROBLOX 44-45

A TALE OF TWO RDCs 46-47

INTRO TO STUDIO 48-49

TOP 10 MOST-PLAYED GAMES ON ROBLOX 50-51

5TH ANNUAL BLOXY AWARDS HIGHLIGHTS 52-53

GAMES YOU MAY HAVE MISSED 54-55

WHOBLOXEDWHO'S FAVORITE GAMES! 56-57

FAMOUS HATS THROUGH THE AGES 58-59

DEVELOPER LESSONS: BUILDING 60-61

ROBLOX MERCH 62-63

TOP 10 MOST-PLAYED GAMES ON ROBLOX 64-65

RECAP QUIZ 66-67

SEE YOU ON ROBLOX! 68-69

INTRODUCTION

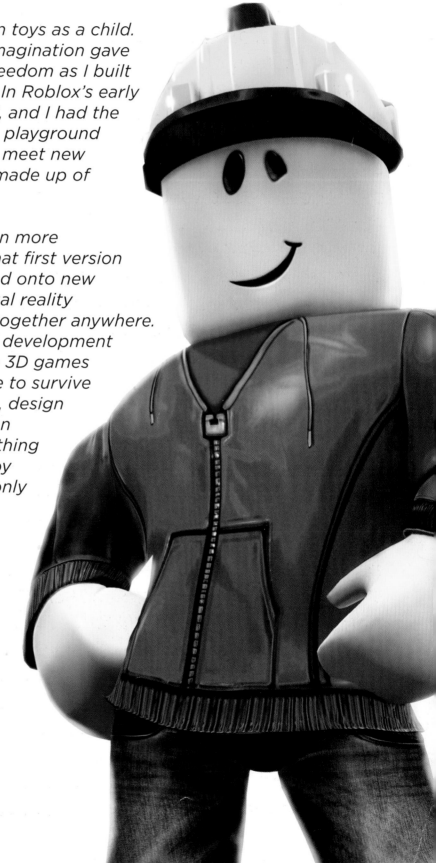

I loved playing with construction toys as a child. Being creative and using my imagination gave me an unparalleled sense of freedom as I built cars, rockets, houses, and bridges. In Roblox's early history, our co-founder, Erik Cassel, and I had the vision to create the ultimate online playground where anyone could play together, meet new friends, and build their own place made up of thousands of virtual blocks.

Roblox has evolved to become even more immersive and more social since that first version over ten years ago. We've expanded onto new devices, from smartphones to virtual reality headsets, allowing friends to play together anywhere. And we continue to provide better development tools so players like you can create 3D games and experiences where it's possible to survive a natural disaster with your friends, design roller coasters, compete in a fashion show, and so much more. But one thing hasn't changed — and that is the joy you feel from building something only you could have imagined.

Without further ado, I leave you to enjoy this comprehensive journey into Roblox's rich history, shining a spotlight on the incredible community and world we have built together.

Sincerely,
David Baszucki, a.k.a. Builderman

MEET SOME OF THE ROBLOX FAMILY

There are millions of Robloxians to meet and plenty of time to meet them, but there are a few very special individuals that you should know from the outset – The Roblox Family! Read on to meet six of the bravest, most innovative, and most powerful residents of Robloxia.

BUILDERMAN

He's the original avatar of David Baszucki, CEO and co-founder of the ultimate Imagination Platform, and an inspiration for creators the world over. In the early days, Builderman, along with the rest of the Roblox team, helped to create iconic games like Crossroads, but now he concentrates on enabling a new generation of creators to become game development superstars.

EZEBEL: THE PIRATE QUEEN

Her name gives away her standing, but once upon a time Ezebel was an excellent student who graduated at the top of her class. She had the world at her feet, but chose to commandeer a band of buccaneers and sail the world, striking fear into all who crossed her. Ez has dominion over the seven seas and nothing happens on them unless she's been consulted first.

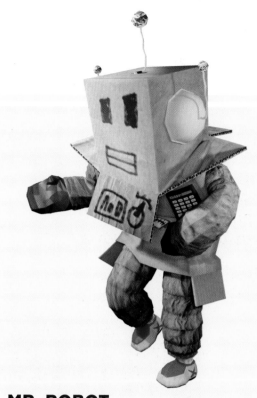

MR. ROBOT

Nobody knows whether Mr. Robot was born or manufactured, nor could they tell you who exactly hides beneath his low-tech helmet. Despite the mystery surrounding his origin and identity, Robloxia has welcomed him with open arms.

MR. BLING BLING

The embodiment of glamor, Mr. Bling Bling is as flamboyant as they come – his sparkling smile and fabulous suit ensure he stands out from the crowd. What he lacks in subtlety, he makes up for in charm, and he will gladly tell of his extravagant lifestyle.

REDCLIFF ELITE COMMANDER

Duty bound to rid the land of all evil, Redcliff Elite Commander has proven to be a brave and powerful warrior. Having risen through the ranks of the Redcliff military, he now leads an elite legion of knights against the evil Korblox empire.

CLASSIC NOOB

Classic Noob is the hapless younger brother of the family, causing harm where he means to do good, taking wrong turns when he should go straight, and leaving chaos in his wake. Although he's prone to panic, he's a loyal friend to all Robloxians.

ROBLOX RETROSPECTIVE

Doesn't time fly when you're having fun? Roblox has been powering imagination for over twelve years, but its origin story goes back even further than that – all the way to 1989. Let us take a journey down memory lane to discover its history ...

Friends Erik Cassel and David Baszucki started work on Interactive Physics, which allowed students to create 2D physics experiments on their computers. This piece of software sparked Erik's and Dave's Robloxian imaginations.

Roblox was starting to take shape and grow very quickly. Erik and Dave were joined by John Shedletsky and Matt Dusek, who became the first Roblox employees.

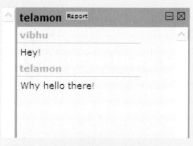

The team at Roblox HQ introduced the Live Chat system, which allowed gamers to talk to each other within the Roblox platform.

1989 — **2006** — **2007** — **2009**

Fast forward a decade, and Erik and David began their epic journey. In a tiny office in Menlo Park, they started to expand on their vision and began developing the software that eventually became Roblox.

A new virtual economy system was released, which allowed users to purchase a variety of items that could be used to customize their own avatars.

The first version of Roblox was launched! It was very simple, with limited characters and only three games available, including classics like Crossroads.

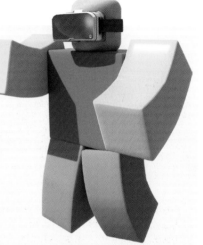

Roblox broke new frontiers when the Roblox app was released on smartphones. A year later, Roblox was released on iPad, allowing gamers to play their favorite Roblox games on the move!

Roblox made the leap from desktop to console, allowing Robloxians to play their favorite Roblox games on Xbox One!

Roblox stepped into the future of gaming with its release of Roblox VR, which allowed gamers to use new virtual reality headsets.

2011 — **2013** — **2015** — **2016**

Roblox launched the DevEx program, allowing developers to change Robux into real bucks. This meant that creators could turn the money that users spent in their games into real cash.

Roblox swapped the previous blocky landscape for "Smooth Terrain," which allowed the creation of easily manipulated and highly textured landscapes. Roblox also added lots of new tools to Studio to make creating places even easier.

The new and improved R15 avatar was released with 9 more body parts than the R6 avatar, opening the door to more expressive movements and animations.

ANOTHER BREAKOUT YEAR!

It's been another historic twelve months in Robloxia, packed full of memorable moments, new features, and record-breaking achievements. In that time, Roblox has changed the way we play together, and crafted new tools for innovative developers to build better experiences! Here's the lowdown of the last year in Robloxia.

A WORLD OF PLAYERS

In a few short years, Roblox has attracted a staggering number of new players to its wonderful world of exciting games, interesting places, and epic experiences! Over the past twelve months, the number of monthly gamers soared to over sixty million! That's quite a few new Robloxians to meet and greet.

PLAYING TOGETHER

Playing together on Roblox has never been easier with new cross-platform capabilities, giving friends the opportunity to co-experience on Xbox One, PC, Mac, and mobile devices. This led to over two million simultaneous users playing together on Roblox at peak times during the year.

STUDIO STYLE

Roblox is all about user-generated content and the stories, worlds, and characters that are created by many talented developers. To help them out, Roblox Studio was upgraded with new features, including a revamped pathfinding system, inverse kinematics for constraints, and glass material objects.

DEVELOPER REVOLUTION

The team at Roblox knows how important creative developers are to the success of the platform. As with every year, these developers are pushing boundaries, pioneering new approaches, and being outrageously inventive! Some top developers are able to work full-time creating games, with many of the most successful earning around $3 million a year through the DevEx program.

EXTRA EMPLOYEES

Roblox HQ was getting a little tight! The team of super staff doubled in size (numbers-wise; they didn't grow into giants) and were too squeezed in the old offices. So Roblox relocated to a bigger, brighter, and more awesome office – the perfect place for interns to come and learn!

TOY STORIES

The vast Robloxian ecosystem of great games and fantastic characters spread beyond the digital realm and escaped into the real world! The new awesome Roblox action figures have been flying off the shelves, as has an apparel line. You may have noticed that a couple of cool books have been released too!

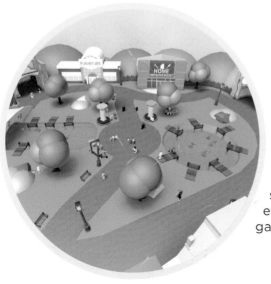

BILLIONAIRE

A momentous milestone was reached within the last year when Alexnewtron's MeepCity hit a record-shattering one billion visits! What makes this landmark even more amazing is the fact that the social hangout game was only created in 2016!

FIRST DAY IN ROBLOX

So you've decided to join Roblox to play and create games with millions of fellow Robloxians? Smart choice – but the platform's sheer magnitude of depth could be a little bit overwhelming to wrap your head around. Follow the advice in this handy guide to sample everything that Roblox has to offer in your first 24 hours.

1

What better way to familiarize yourself with Roblox than by playing a game? Head to the Games page to choose one of millions, from dozens of genres. If you like a game, add it to your Favorites list by clicking the star on the individual game page.

MEEPCITY

WORK AT A PIZZA PLACE

2

When you head back to the landing page, you'll see your avatar's headshot, but it looks a bit ... well, ordinary. Enter the Catalog area, where you can browse and buy clothes and accessories. You can buy items with Robux, or find free ones instead.

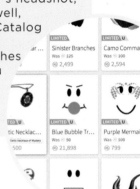

4

We all know playing games is better with friends, so it's time to create your Friends list. Find out your friends' usernames and search for them. From their Player page, click the Add Friend button to send them a request, or send them a message once they accept.

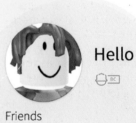
Hello

Friends

3

Now to personalize your character in the Avatar section. Using the Avatar Editor, you can try on the items bought from the Catalog to find the best combo, as well as choosing model type, height, width, head size, and body proportions. Much better!

5

Once you've added all your friends, you can chat with them from within the Roblox site. Click the Play Together button at the top of a chat window to turn the group into a Party. The window will turn green, and you can search for games to play together.

Dec 6, 2017 | 1

hello

6

No matter when you join, there's probably an event going on, which can reward you with exclusive loot, avatar items, and badges just for taking part and playing an awesome Roblox game. Sounds like the perfect activity for your Party to get involved in!

ROBLOX SUMMER GAMES

7

You'll quickly realize that the community is what makes Roblox so special. Become a part of it by joining one of the lively Groups. Whatever you're interested in – art, game development, clan warfare, or just a specific game – there's a group of like-minded Robloxians who'll warmly welcome you.

MEDIEVAL WARFARE: REFORGED

APOCALYPSE RISING

JAILBREAK

8

Why not get a taste for the Studio side of Roblox, where you can create your own worlds and games? You don't need to know how to program, just load a baseplate, play with some free models, and try out all the different tools.

Start/Finish

9

There's never a dull moment on Roblox, so make sure to check the official Blog often. Whether it's an interview with a top dev, an update on the latest tech, or the fanfare signaling the start of the next movie partnership event, you'll hear the news here first!

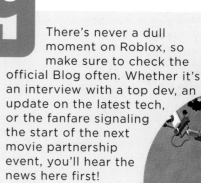

TOP 10 MOST-PLAYED GAMES ON ROBLOX

Roblox is the home of awesome games – millions of them, in fact. To help you discover some of the best it has to offer, we've compiled a top-ten chart of some of Roblox's most popular games. To begin with, we have two games about discovering your true Robloxian self.

10 SUPERHERO TYCOON

As with most tycoon experiences, the aim of this superhero-creator is to build a base by earning cash. At the start, you must claim a vacant base to assume the role of a hero. To earn money to spend on your base, weapons, and superpowers, build as many droppers as possible. As your kills grow, you can test yourself against other players, or engage in an epic battle against a series of superhero bosses.

9 ROBLOXIAN LIFE

When real life gets a little dull, why not spawn into DemSkittlesDoee's role-play classic Robloxian Life! You can live your Robloxian life however you wish; be a parent, teen, kid, or even a pet. Then, once you have found your role in life, explore the world, visit the mall, catch a movie with friends, or even adopt a child! You can even buy a car and cruise around town looking for the perfect place to call home.

ROLE-PLAY

The town map is full of fun places to explore and role-play with your new friends. As a teen, you can attend Robloxian School, catch up with friends in class, and then chill at the mall. Parents can adopt kids, make time for a delicious meal at the restaurant, or keep in perfect bloxy shape at the gym.

POWER DROP

The key mechanic to Superhero Tycoon is earning money. You finance your superhero life by building "droppers" that drop cubes onto a conveyor, amassing you a stream of cash. As you earn money, you can improve your base with walls, doors, and stairs, as well as buy everything you need to be a hero – weapons, powers, and a super costume.

BATTLE ARENA

In between collecting cash and upgrading your base, you can test your superhero mettle against bosses at the arena in the middle of the map. Take them on to practice your heat-ray-vision accuracy or web-slinging prowess.

DEVELOPER

DrFBD

This superhero fan has been part of the Roblox community since 2013. After the success of Superhero Tycoon, he created the game development group Super Studios, which developed the epic battle game Bloc Blitz.

A SUPERHERO QUEST

Players can also earn diamonds by completing quests. These include battling a specific superhero, or going rogue and defeating other gamers in the map. Players can also buy special power perks, weapons, passes, and even superhero sidekicks.

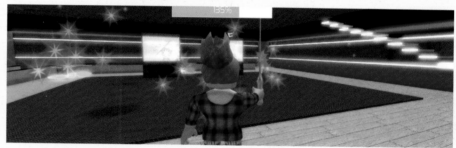

CUSTOMIZE YOUR LIFE

There are lots of things to buy in the game, from apartments and cars to new gear and clothes. You can even choose new dance moves to show off at Club Ruby, or customize your avatar with a completely new look ... like a pet-tastic animal mesh!

LIFE SAVINGS

Like most open-world games on Roblox, you can earn money just by spending time playing the game. Watch your money bar grow and turn to cash that you can splash on all the Robloxian luxuries you need in your new Robloxian life!

DEVELOPER

DemSkittlesDoee

This playful developer has been living life on Roblox since 2012 and has launched his own game creation group Skittle Studios. Among his other games are Boys And Girls Hangout and Bloxy Town.

PIXELATEDCANDY'S FAVORITE GAMES!

PixelatedCandy is always on trend and knows what looks good. She's the developer behind the classic style sensation Fashion Famous! and is the founder of the development group Pixelated Candies, which has over 250,000 members. We tracked her down to discover her favorite Roblox games of all time.

"The moments where you're about to die but somehow survive are the most thrilling parts of the experience."

NATURAL DISASTER SURVIVAL

PixelatedCandy's first choice is Natural Disaster Survival by Stickmasterluke. She loves how the game uses its simplicity to its advantage, and enjoys the challenge of surviving all the different types of disasters, from flash floods to mighty meteor showers.

"I also enjoy the emphasis on teamwork ... you have friends who can help you through the horror around every corner!"

IDENTITY FRAUD

This fashionable developer likes being scared! Her next favorite game is Identity Fraud by Team MOTHERBOARD. She loves how the game combines puzzles, mazes, and shocking scares to create a thrilling and chilling experience!

"I love the concept of making something original ... it felt like my imagination was the only limit I had."

THEME PARK TYCOON 2

Next up on her all-time faves list is Theme Park Tycoon 2 by Den_S. PixelatedCandy is a self-professed fan of the genre from her younger days and loves seeing her park grow as more customers come and enjoy the rides!

"The moments I loved the most were the times where my team would take over other enemy bases and use their loot to our advantage."

APOCALYPSE RISING

PixelatedCandy can also handle herself during a catastrophe! But not of the catwalk kind, more of the horror apocalypse sort. Her next choice of game is the iconic Apocalypse Rising by Gusmanak and ZolarKeth.

"Probably one of the most fun games on Roblox to me because it allows me to experience my childhood fear of the ocean and sharks within a game."

SHARKBITE

Completing PixelatedCandy's ensemble of Roblox faves is Abracadabra's SharkBite. She loves the cutely designed boats and how the game is beautifully balanced, making it fun to play as the shark as well as the gun-toting shark hunters!

AVATAR EVOLUTION

Since the inception of Roblox, the avatar has been a mainstay of the platform. Like most things, however, it has undergone an incredible metamorphosis, from a classic blocky character to a dynamic, customizable persona, available in a variety of body shapes. Here we take a look at the changes the avatar has gone through to make it more versatile than ever.

THE FIRST GENERATION
On the release of Roblox, the avatar was basic – its body, arms, and legs were blocky, and had no hint of hands and feet, nor did it have any animation.

WARDROBE!
In 2007, a year after Roblox was released, users were able to buy clothing created by other users for their avatar to wear.

BODY SWAPPER
Roblox also opened up the potential for body part packages, which allowed users to swap out sets of body parts and customize the shape of their character on a limited scale.

EMOTICON
Roblox also introduced "emotes" for avatars, which users could utilize to wave to and cheer at other players.

GETTING ANIMATED
The R6 avatar, which was split into 6 separate, posable body parts, was released. This avatar began to use the Keyframe Animation system, which allowed for smoother, more realistic movements.

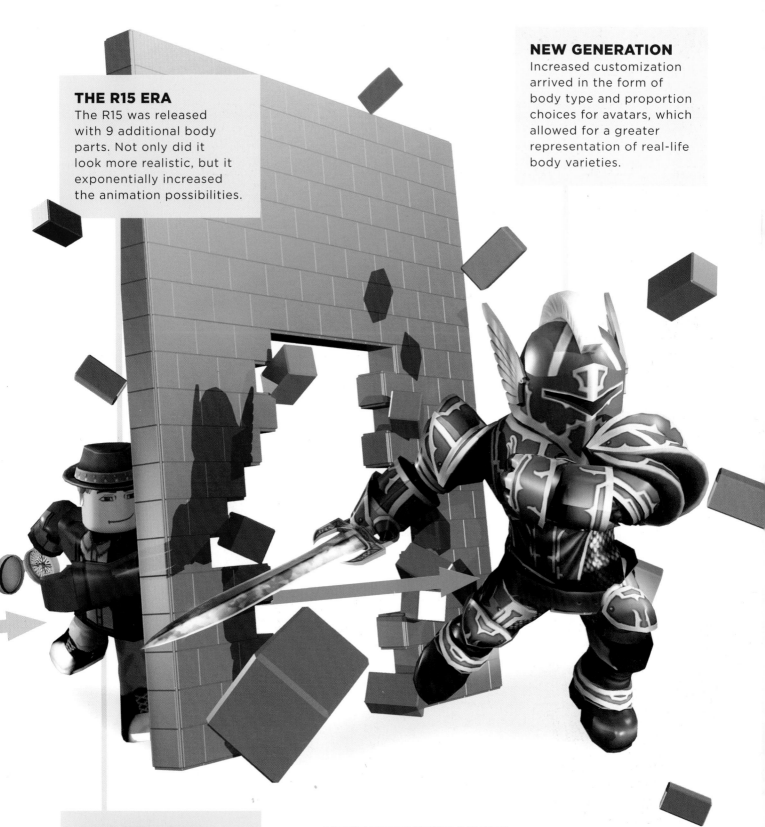

THE R15 ERA
The R15 was released with 9 additional body parts. Not only did it look more realistic, but it exponentially increased the animation possibilities.

NEW GENERATION
Increased customization arrived in the form of body type and proportion choices for avatars, which allowed for a greater representation of real-life body varieties.

CUSTOMIZATION
Support was added to allow users to customize the height, width, and head size of their characters, allowing increased realism or absurdity, depending on how much the scales are played with.

NEXT BREAKTHROUGH?
It's clear to see the great keyframe-animated strides that the avatar has taken in the 12 years that it has been around. But there are still many more steps in the avatar's journey as the team works hard on further upgrades and improvements. For now, we can only dream about the avatar's next metamorphosis.

DEVELOPER LESSONS: GAME DESIGN

You've played games on Roblox, but have you ever thought about making them? Roblox Studio is the perfect introduction to game development, but before you get started you need to design your game! Crazyblox, developer of Flood Escape 2, has offered up his top tips on designing your own game.

SHOW THE WAY

No matter what type of game you're working on, players should always know where they need to go. "This is most commonly done by using arrows to point people in the right direction," says Crazyblox. A subtler approach might involve having a wire lead from a secret button to the door that it opens. In open world games, you can use markers on a map or quest bubbles over a character's head.

CREATING INTERESTING MECHANICS

Game mechanics describe how players interact with a game. Most games have mechanics like walking or flying, but it could also include solving puzzles, growing plants, or digging for gold. Players should have to use the game mechanics to overcome challenges. Some mechanics used by Crazyblox in Flood Escape 2 include swimming, pressing buttons to unlock gates, and jumping onto platforms to avoid the rising water.

ENCOURAGE TEAM PLAY

Flood Escape 2 encourages team play to succeed, so it's important to reward individual players for working together. Crazyblox accomplishes this by "rewarding players with XP for making use of game mechanics." This gives players an incentive to keep going and help the team reach the next stage.

SHOW IMPORTANT INFO

The graphical user interface, or GUI, provides players with information about the game such as their health, points, and resources. In Flood Escape 2, the GUI displays an "air bar" that shows the player their remaining air when they're underwater. In the lobby, it switches back to displaying level and XP information. Crazyblox says that this decision was made because "it would be difficult to show all the information without cluttering the screen."

MAKE HAZARDS OBVIOUS

Hazards are a good way to create challenges for the players to overcome. "The biggest hazard in Flood Escape 2 is running out of air. There's also lava that drowns the player instantly," says Crazyblox. Your players will be unhappy if they die without warning, so communicating danger with color and sound is important. Bright red colors make lava obviously dangerous, and muffling music lets players know when they're underwater and might drown.

PLATFORMER

One of the best things about Roblox is that you can play it ANYWHERE! You can play at your desk on PC and Mac, from the sofa on Xbox One or Oculus Rift, or while you're on the move using a smartphone or tablet! Here's a list of tips to maximize the Roblox experience on each platform.

PC/MAC

The original home of Roblox, the desktop version is the most fully featured of all Roblox packages. As well as having access to millions of games, Robloxians can also take advantage of Roblox Studio and make their own game! You can even play in VR on Oculus Rift.

PLAY ALL THE GAMES
The desktop version of Roblox has access to a large majority of titles, from shooters and role-playing games, to obbys and infinite runners. No matter what games you like, you'll find plenty of amazing games to play here.

TRY BUILDING
Playing games is great, but you can really let your imagination go by building games in Roblox Studio. You don't need to know how to code – load up a template, customize, and share.

XBOX ONE

The first console incarnation of the world's most popular entertainment platform for play launched in 2015 with 15 games available. The gamut of games has grown exponentially since then, with hundreds of popular devs making their games available to millions of console owners.

TAKE CONTROL
You can set up some controllers to work with the desktop version of Roblox, but if you want instant access to your favorite games with a controller, you can make the jump to Xbox One instead. All you need is a comfy chair, and you're set!

SHOW OFF
Are you on a hot streak on Speed Run 4? Or maybe you're maxing out your K/D Ratio on Phantom Forces? You should show everyone how good you are – press the Xbox button and then Y to record the last thirty seconds, or X to capture a screenshot.

MOBILE

Why should you have to leave the world of Roblox behind just because you leave the house? Fortunately, you don't have to – Roblox is available on Android and iOS devices, and Amazon's line of Kindles, so you can pick up your game when you're out and about.

AVATAR CREATION

Sometimes, choosing the right outfit to wear (not to mention your three best hats) can take hours. The app has a handy avatar editor that allows you to quickly swap out all your available avatar items and design a new style in minutes.

CHAT HUB

As well as being perfect for mobile entertainment, the handheld version of the app can serve as a chat hub while you're playing another version of Roblox. This keeps your main screen free and focused on your objective, while you organize your party via a group on the app.

WHERE TO GET ROBLOX

If you don't already have Roblox (and why not!), you can pick it up from any of the following outlets. You can download desktop versions from the Roblox website, get Xbox and desktop versions from Microsoft Store and get it for mobile devices on the App Store®, Google Play and Amazon.

GAMES YOU MAY HAVE MISSED

With over 40 million games and places to visit on Roblox, it's understandable if a few games have flown under your radar. Don't worry, we're here to give you a top-secret briefing on games that may have gone undetected. Read these profiles, then check out these hidden gems.

ROYALE HIGH

This open world is full of fantastical high school fun! Claim a locker and dorm room in the fairy-tale castle before venturing into a world of happily-ever-after. Attend classes to boost your grades and earn diamonds, which you can use to customize every part of your high school experience.

LEARN AND EARN
Keep an eye on the schedule and get to class on time! As you ace subjects, including enchanted art and potions chemistry, you earn diamonds, which you can spend on your character and dorm room.

YOUR OWN KING-DORM
Head to the top of the castle to find and claim your own dorm room. Once you've found one, you can style it with furniture and use the closet to find the perfect style to wear to class!

Developer

callmehbob

This regal developer has been wandering through the wonderful kingdom of Roblox for over ten years and hit true royal standing in 2017 with her role-play creation, Royale High.

FRAMED!

Live life as a spy in this espionage thriller! You must use all your covert wiles to evade your enemy as you search for players to eliminate. With just a PDA, luger, knife, and glass of water, you'll need to use your wits to survive the map. You need to watch out for cops and an undercover agent, who can stop you in your tracks if they catch you red-handed!

YOU'VE BEEN FRAMED!

As a framed agent, all you have to help find your target is a picture of their face. The game becomes a spy vs. spy affair as players await the ideal time to take out their target, keeping an eye out for the agent after them!

A THIN BLUE LINE

Rounds have two cops and an undercover agent. As cops, you must work as a team to hunt each framed agent. You need patience and a keen eye because framed players can only be eliminated if they're caught with a gun, or if they kil! the wrong target!

TIP... The classic Framed! mode is a great experience, but the spy games don't stop there. Other modes are available, such as City Chase, where teams of cops and agents battle it out in a city map, and Double Agents, which pits undercover agents against the framed players in a cat-and-mouse thriller!

Developer
pa00

This snake-wearing developer is a former Roblox intern and has been playing and making games since 2010. His other classic games include Legendary: The Necromancer's Revenge and Frenzy.

RICKYTHEFISHY'S FAVORITE GAMES!

The next developer top-five comes from marine-loving dev RickyTheFishy. This aquatic programmer is the big fish behind Fish Simulator, and is the founder of development group Shark Fin Studios. He's been lurking in the depths of Roblox since 2014, and has hauled in a few awesome games along the way.

1

> "My all-time favorite game on Roblox is Lumber Tycoon 2, because it's such a simple concept."

LUMBER TYCOON 2

RickyTheFishy's first catch of the day is Defaultio's woodchopper sim, Lumber Tycoon 2. He loves the game's engaging simplicity and captivating mix of tycoon-management and ingenious game quests.

> "A truly entertaining experience for a wide range of players."

PRISON LIFE

Next up for this oceanic coder is the much-loved, much-played escapist classic, Prison Life. RickyTheFishy loves the minimalist style and how it proves that sometimes simplicity—in design, building, and gameplay—can create an engaging and fascinating gaming experience.

2

"I love being the shark and cruising around ..."

SHARKBITE

RickyTheFishy's next choice for all-time top game is no surprise. Number three is SharkBite by Abracadabra Studio. This popular survival experience reminds him of his own classic marine game, Fish Simulator, but with a different sharky spin to the gameplay.

"It'll always be the classic of Roblox."

NATURAL DISASTER SURVIVAL

Coming in at number four in RickyTheFishy's all-time Roblox experiences is a favorite among many developers and gamers alike, Natural Disaster Survival. It's a game that never gets boring and can be played over and over again ... it's a true survivor!

"Cube Eat Cube is the game that I always go to whenever I feel adventurous."

CUBE EAT CUBE

Last on the list of great games is Stickmasterluke's addictive Cube Eat Cube. RickyTheFishy loves going back to this minimalist classic and ends up playing it hours on end, trying to eat his way to a high cube number so he can wreak his revenge on the hungry cubes that previously chomped him!

ROBLOX GALLERY OF IMAGINATION

Roblox is full of awesome content, and each game, showcase, and place has its own style that sets it apart from the rest. Here's a selection of incredible examples of individual style, which shows what you can create using the power of imagination, a few blocks, polygons, and a well-thought-out color scheme.

The hexagonal tiles and colorful maps of this run-and-survive game give it a playful, geometric style.

ARCHMAGE
NEGATIVE GAMES
2017

The cubic-block feel and simple colors of this survival game demonstrate a sleek, structured design.

DISASTER ISLAND
DISASTER ISLAND DEVELOPMENT TEAM
2016

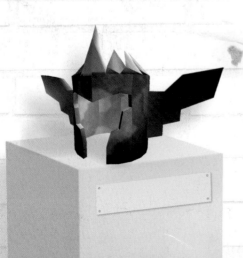

The colorful wireframe design gives this quirky obby game an 80s retro-gaming aesthetic.

GRAVITY SHIFT
MEGUY1
2012

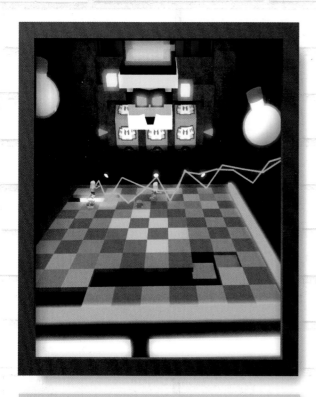

This action-adventure game is stacked full of magical characters and fantastical locations.

FANTASTIC FRONTIER
SPECTRABOX
2016

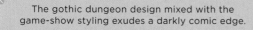

The gothic dungeon design mixed with the game-show styling exudes a darkly comic edge.

DUNGEON MASTER
SHARKBYTE STUDIOS
2017

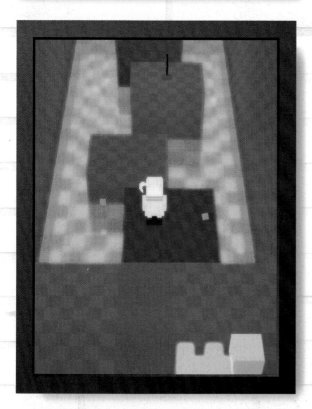

The ultra-detailed, sci-fi design gives this facility a chilling and intriguing realism.

INNOVATION ARCTIC FACILITY
INNOVATION INC.
2017

This bloxy adventure-puzzle game with its pixelated GUI emotes an old-school arcade game feel.

RAMONA
CAPTAIN_ARR'S PARTY
2017

HOTTEST ROBLOX TRENDS

Bored with your avatar's style? Got a few Robux to spend but don't know what's trendy? Well, we have a list of the most popular items from the Catalog to put your finger back on the fashion pulse. None of these items will make you a better gamer, but you'll look good as you respawn for the tenth time ...

PACKAGES

SNOW GENTLEMAN

What's special about a snowman? Kids build them all the time! If you want to look cool as ice, then go the extra-special mile and adopt the dapper Snow Gentleman look!

PENGUIN

Do you strut with a waddle? Then this frosty new look is perfect for you. If you want to flip a flipper and glide with style, then head to the Catalog and pick up a penguin!

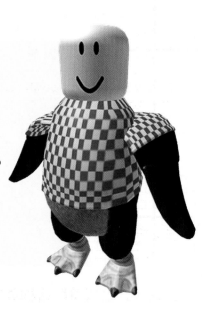

SKELETON

Sometimes your wardrobe can have too much choice. When this happens, go minimal, and strip your style right back to the bare bones for the skeleton look.

KORBLOX MAGE

Ever had those days when you feel a little dark magic will just make everything a little brighter? The Korblox Mage style will do just that, and give you a dark edge.

ACCESSORIES

SHOULDER SLOTH

Shoulder pads are so last century, so try the brand-new trend making waves in fashion ... the draped-pet look! This is perfect for Robloxians who live life in the slow lane.

XTREME RAINBOW HAIR

Brighten everyone's day with this extravagant hairstyle! Come rain or shine, it will make you feel like you can walk on clouds, and pairs well with a wide spectrum of styles!

WATERMELON SHARK

Just when you thought it was safe to go back into the fruit bowl! This marine-melon look is the perfect accessory for anyone hoping to add a tasty bite to their fashion ensemble.

JOHN'S GLASSES

Imagine a world where you don't own a piece of iconic rockstar apparel – terrible, isn't it? Grab these iconic glasses and you'll look good even after a hard day's night spent on Roblox!

GEAR

DANGEROUS AXEPACK

Made with fine Robloxian steel and crafted by the masters of an ancient volcanic forge, these axes are the strongest in the land ... but just in case one breaks, you've got a spare to wield!

DARKAGE NINJA SWORDPACK

You can never have too many sharp things strapped to your back! Just in case the age of darkness arrives unexpectedly, there's no harm in being prepared with this swordpack!

GRAVITY COIL

One thing that can really drag you down is gravity! Use the gravity coil to combat gravity's grounding power in certain games, allowing you to jump extra high or fall like a feather!

BODY SWAP POTION

Even with a full wardrobe, you'll often get envious of others' outfits. This magic elixir is the perfect remedy, and will grant you the chance to step into another player's shoes.

TOP 10 MOST-PLAYED GAMES ON ROBLOX

Our next stops on the most-played countdown take in two classics, whose popularity resonates with fellow devs just as much as the wider Robloxian community. So, hold onto your hat and get ready for a tornado, or skulk in the shadows for a deadly game of cat-and-mouse.

8 ASSASSIN!

Do you have what it takes to be a top hitman? Can you stealthily track a target and pick the right time to attack, all the while looking over your own shoulder? If so, this game is perfect for you. In prisman's Assassin!, players enter one of the many beautifully crafted maps and are given a target to pick off with their knife, all the while keeping a lookout for the assassin that has them in their sights!

7 NATURAL DISASTER SURVIVAL

Are you a natural born survivor? Ever braved a nasty storm or dealt with a hair-rufflingly windy day? If that sounds like you, then Stickmasterluke's Natural Disaster Survival is right up your meteorological street. With a wide array of disasters to outwit and an archipelago of island maps to experience, you can see why this survival game has maintained its popularity for over a decade!

WHAT A DISASTER!
One disaster looks pretty much like another disaster, right? Wrong. In Natural Disaster Survival, there are over ten very different disasters to endure, from sandstorms and acid rain to erupting volcanoes and meteor showers. Each disaster has its own unique pattern to work out and outwit, so keep an eye on the forecast!

HIT JOB

Assassin! is part of a popular hunt-and-eliminate genre that also includes games such as Framed!. All of them have their own twist, and in Assassin! it's a simple hitman vs. hitman mission. As you track down your target and pick them off with your knife, you'll receive a new target until you are the last player standing and can savor the victory of survival!

KNOW YOUR KNIFE

When you start, you're given a basic knife to help in your trade as assassin extraordinaire. As you progress through the levels and earn tokens for your awesome skills, you can upgrade your knife, making you even more deadly.

DEVELOPER

prisman

This purple-clad developer has been creating awesome content on Roblox since 2016, and his classic creation Assassin! has clocked up over 300 million visits to date.

CRAFTING

A cool feature allows players to use a crafting area to create new weapons. Players can merge together different types of blades to fashion a more formidable knife, allowing them to earn more tokens and experience points within the various arenas.

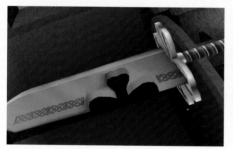

MAPPING SURVIVAL

As with many games in the survival genre, the art of survival is affected by the map you play. There are over fifteen maps on which you may find yourself searching for cover, with race tracks, amusement parks, and skyscrapers all offering their own survival solutions ... and problems.

KNOW YOUR DISASTER

To be a true survivor, a player needs to learn how each disaster works to plot a survival masterplan. Some require a jumpy sprint to the tallest tower, while for others sheltering under the stairs will suffice. However, with any plan, a little bit of luck always comes in handy!

DEVELOPER

Stickmasterluke

This developer extraordinaire has been surviving on Roblox since 2007 and has created some of Roblox's most addictive games, including The Underground War and Cube Eat Cube.

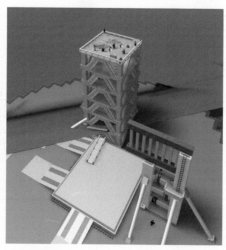

ROBLOX CALENDAR

No matter what time of year it is, there's always an event to get excited about and take part in on Roblox. This calendar shows off just twelve months' worth of events that players were able to take part in and grab exclusive event loot and badges.

THE BLOXYS

The new year was ushered in with style at the Bloxys, the annual celebration of the most incredible achievements on Roblox over the past 12 months. Many users got their hands on a ticket for the ceremony, or tuned in to the live stream to see the winners!

HEROES

Robloxians assemble! This superpowered occasion was full of disaster aversion, action, and exclusive loot! Team Super's Heroes of Robloxia was first released as part of this event – does this mean we can expect more super-exclusive games from future events?

JANUARY

 MARCH

FEBRUARY

 APRIL

 MAY

 **JUNE**

EGG HUNT

The arrival of spring brought with it the legendary quest for ovoid artifacts and another chance to save the Eggverse from evil. The search often yielded egg-citing avatar rewards to those who collected the most eggs.

RDC

The Roblox Developers Conference brought together the greatest dev minds on the platform. The event was filled with exciting presentations, game jams, tournaments, and much more. Keep your fingers crossed for an invite to the next exclusive event.

As well as seasonal events, look out for themed events that pop up throughout the year:

Innovation
An event suited to tinkerers, gadgeteers, and artisans, this platform-spanning showcase handed out exclusive items for completing tasks in the most popular games revolving around crafting and creating.

Universe
Players explored cosmic frontiers and collected goodies along the way in the star-tripping Universe event. Completing in-game quests rewarded space-age weaponry, wings, and outfits.

Imagination
A celebration of the boundaries that the Roblox community are pushing and, in some instances, breaking. Rewards were up for grabs in some of the most ingenious games on the platform.

NIGHTMARE BEFORE BLOXTOBER/ HALLOW'S EVE

During the time of year when things start to go bump in the night, players joined in the fun on Roblox with the Nightmare Before Bloxtober and Hallow's Eve events. Spooky avatar items were offered to participants, meaning the scares could continue all year!

WINTER GAMES

The chilly, snow-covered cousin of the Summer Games was no less fun. The final event of the year offered a similar bevy of exclusive rewards for completing wintry missions within some of the best games, but without running the risk of frostbite.

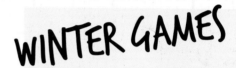

JULY

AUGUST

SEPTEMBER

OCTOBER

NOVEMBER

DECEMBER

SUMMER GAMES

When the sun reached its zenith around the middle of the year, it heralded the start of the Summer Games. Players donned shades and caps to get ready for this event, which featured a handful of games and objectives to be completed in order to win exclusive avatar items.

BLOXGIVING

Users gave thanks for Roblox and its myriad of awesome games in the Bloxgiving event. As usual, there were quests to complete in a host of Thanksgiving-themed games, which rewarded players with a bunch of themed avatar items.

5TH ANNUAL BLOXY AWARDS HIGHLIGHTS

Every young Robloxian dreams of a nomination at the Bloxy Awards. They celebrate the highest echelon of excellence in Roblox, including the year's best games and developers, stand-out community stars, and ingenious innovators. The winners are generally decided by the community but there are also awards based on data, such as playtime and visits. Here are a few stellar highlights from the red carpet of the 5th Annual Bloxy Awards!

BUILDER OF THE YEAR

GAME OF THE YEAR

Jailbreak
Badimo's hugely popular escape game won the coveted Game of the Year award and was the overwhelming success story of the Bloxys, taking home a total of nine shiny statues!

BUILDER OF THE YEAR

DieSoft
This elite builder of Robloxia scooped up this award for his awesome world-crafting skills. As a fitting reward, his development group, Nocturne Entertainment, was given the honor of building the ceremony theater that hosted the Bloxys!

STUDIO OF THE YEAR

Badimo
This duo stole the show at the awards with their hit game Jailbreak. Asimo3089 also won for best original character, and he picked up the award for most popular Roblox toy!

MOBILE GAME OF THE YEAR

MeepCity
With Roblox pushing barriers on mobile gaming, this award went to a game that has also broken new ground on the platform – Alexnewtron's much-visited, much-loved MeepCity!

LIFETIME ACHIEVEMENT AWARD

Stickmasterluke
This was awarded to a Roblox veteran who joined in 2007, and has created some of the most classic experiences on Roblox, including Natural Disaster Survival and Cube Eat Cube.

XBOX GAME OF THE YEAR

Design It!
This new category was created to highlight the success of Roblox on its newest platform, and the inaugural winner was the fashion-challenge game Design It! by tktech.

BEST TEAM-BASED MULTIPLAYER GAME

Flood Escape 2
The Bloxy for best team-based experience went to Crazyblox Games' Flood Escape 2. This survival game sees teams trying to flee the floodwater by running, swimming, and climbing to high ground.

BUILDERMAN AWARD FOR EXCELLENCE

Jailbreak
Won by some legendary Robloxians in the past, this year's award, presented by Builderman himself, went to the breakout stars of the ceremony, Badimo, and their hit game Jailbreak.

MORE AWARDS

Favorite Breakout Game
Jailbreak

Favorite Updated Game
Welcome to Bloxburg

Best Free-For-All Multiplayer Game
Epic Minigames

Best Art Direction
Dance Your Blox Off

Best Tutorial
Restaurant Tycoon

Quirkiest Game
Eat or Die

Video of the Year
Alone

Most Concurrents: Desktop/Xbox
Jailbreak

Most Concurrents: Mobile
MeepCity

Most Concurrents Overall
Jailbreak

Games You've Spent The Most Hours Playing
Jailbreak

High Rated
Welcome to Bloxburg

Most VIP Servers
Jailbreak

Most Returning
Welcome to Bloxburg

Most Visits: Desktop
Jailbreak

Most Visits: Mobile
MeepCity

Most Visits Overall
Jailbreak

Best Use of Physics
Gravity Shift

Best Single Player Game
The Ink Workshop

Hardest Roblox Game
Escape Room

GAMES YOU MAY HAVE MISSED

Here are some more super-awesome games that may have evaded your keen Roblox recon skills. With new gaming treasures to discover every day, you've got to keep your ear to the ground. Quickly read and memorize the briefings below as this page will self-destruct in five, four, three ... only kidding.

DRAGON RAGE

Get your jumpsuits ready, secure your helmet, and prepare for a survival showdown with some large, scaly beasts! Dragon Rage, created by TigerCode, is a fun survival game with some flying fantasy fiends to avoid in an epic game of dodge-the-dragons. Gamers spawn into one of the many island maps that offer seemingly safe high ground, but watch the skies as the dragons swoop and destroy the land, forcing gamers into the surrounding deadly waters.

DRAGON SKIES
Dragon Rage could be considered to be a "survival of the highest" game. As players leap, run, and swim to safety, they must keep one eye on the skies because more and more dragons will appear and torpedo the island, leaving ever-fewer sanctuaries for the players to hide in.

LEAP DRAGON
Jumping and luck are the keys to survival! Gamers must use the double-jump skill to move across high ground and reach areas of the map that keep their feet dry. Watch out for dive-bombing dragons as they pack a fiery punch that can throw players into the watery depths.

Developer
TigerCode

This fantastical developer has been active on Roblox since 2009 and is part of the development team Silver Fin Studios. In addition to Dragon Rage, the team is behind the classic games Blox Hunt and Christmas Rush.

SHARKBITE

This survival game has only been on Roblox since early 2017 but has already attracted many fans across the platform! Players enter the lighthouse lobby and wait to see if they will be the shark in the next game. Once the shark has been chosen, the other players choose a boat and invite fellow sailors to join their shark-hunting expedition.

IT'S A SHARK'S LIFE

Each time you play, someone assumes the role of the shark, and each session you complete increases your chance of becoming the megalodon menace. As the giant-jawed monster, you must swim around looking for survivors to munch and boats to capsize, as you dodge bullets from gun-toting hunters.

WE NEED A BIGGER BOAT

As a survivor, your first action is to choose your own boat or join another player's hunting party. There are several seaworthy vessels to choose from, including a speedboat, a pleasure yacht, and a fancy duck boat. The more players you can get on your crew, the more firepower you have against the shark!

TIP... This might sound pretty obvious ... and it kind of is ... but the top tip is don't go in the water. The boats can get crowded and zip along at top speed, so if you topple overboard you may find yourself adrift in the water with a large, shark-sized shadow closing in from the deep!

Developer
Abracadabra Studio

Abracadabra Studio is a game creation group owned by opplo and Simoon68. Both have been sailing the Robloxian seas for nearly ten years, and their hit game SharkBite has attracted over 50 million visits to date.

INSIDE ROBLOX HQ

Ever wondered what it's like inside Roblox's central hub? Well get ready for a grand tour of the shiny new Roblox HQ as we take you inside the walls of their brand new headquarters located in San Mateo, California.

LOBBY

Walk through the front doors of Roblox HQ and you'll find yourself in the lobby area. Here you can mosey around and take a look at the showcases full of Roblox toys, a wall of patents awarded to Builderman and other Roblox team members, and check out the live screen showing how many people are playing Roblox in real-time!

PHOTO BOOTH

Visitors are able to take home a memento of their trip to the central hub of Robloxia by hopping in the lobby's photo booth, striking fun poses, and snapping some pictures to take away with them.

GAMES ROOM

As well as being masters of digital games on the Roblox platform, many team members also love to spend their lunch break engaging their colleagues in classic board games. Workplace rivalries have been forged and settled over legendary games such as Catan and Carcassonne.

LOUNGE

Keeping the biggest online social gaming platform going is hard work, so the site is peppered with lounge areas where staff can go to chill out and relax between bouts of debugging, lengthy meetings, or to congregate with fellow Robloxians for a laid-back catch-up. There's even an awesome veranda so that staff can bask in the California sunshine.

TEAM

The Roblox team is made up of hundreds of people and split across multiple floors. On the top floor of the building you'll find the Engineering team, which keeps the platform working and checks out all the new games appearing on Roblox.

STUDIO

Roblox HQ even has its very own studio, where videos are created for the community. This is where some of the 5th Annual Bloxys were filmed, so it is already a part of Roblox history, even though it's very new.

TOP 10 MOST-PLAYED GAMES ON ROBLOX

In the next two slots of our top-game chart countdown, we have a couple of games full of school shenanigans, skateboards, and part-time jobs! So practice your high school swagger and rev the engine on your delivery scooter!

6 ROBLOX HIGH SCHOOL

Roblox High School comes from developer Cindering and offers an open-world experience for gamers to socialize, explore, and role-play. You can become a part of eight possible cliques, including the teachers, students, and cheerleaders. Once you've joined a clique, the high school campus is your playground to explore with your new buddies, unless you want to go to class and learn something?

5 WORK AT A PIZZA PLACE

It's time to earn some money, so why not work at a pizza place like Builder Brothers Pizza? But what type of job are you going to do? Cashier? Cook? Maybe you're a great pizza-boxer, or your skills lie in being the cool delivery guy. Work at a Pizza Place is full of fun minigames where teamwork is key and employee superstars may get promoted to manager!

COOK IT, BOX IT, DELIVER IT

Each role at Builder Brothers Pizza has its own little mini game. As the cook, you've got to keep an eye on the orders, build the pizzas, and make sure you don't overcook them in the ovens! Boxers need to box up the perfectly crafted pizzas, and the delivery team gets to drive them around town!

SKATE AND PLAY

When you're in high school, the days go on forever! Which is great in Roblox High School because it means you can hit the skate park, chat with some cheerleaders before diving into the swimming pool, and then it's time for a big night out at Club Red. And don't forget your favorite class in the Computer Lab!

HOME SWEET HOME

You don't just hang at school in this open-world game. You can also get a house, and buy furniture, new clothes, and gear. You can even purchase a pet! If the great outdoors is more your style, why not rent a cabin in the forest?

AFTER SCHOOL JOB

Making money in Roblox High School is a matter of patience, since you earn money as the clock ticks. But if your attention span is limited and you need more cash, grab your fishing rod and go catch some fish. Soon you'll be looking flash with the cash and maybe even get a car!

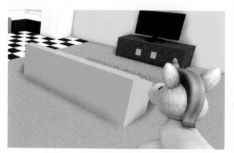

DEVELOPER

Cindering

The award-winning Cindering has been making games on Roblox since 2009 and was part of the Roblox Ambassador program. Another one of his games is Sharpshooter Mines, a frantic mine-and-battle survival game.

MANAGER'S OFFICE

Every pizza place has a manager in charge of the team. They have to make sure the pizza place runs smoothly, keep an eye on all the employees, and if there are some star performers, they can hand out bonuses! But watch out, if the workforce gets restless, bad bosses can get fired!

THERE'S NO "ME" IN PIZZA

Work at a Pizza Place is all about teamwork. If the cashier doesn't take the order, or the delivery guy gets lost, then no one is going to get paid, let alone get their hands on a bonus! Also, be sure to keep an eye on the supplies ... no supplies means no pizza, and no pizza means no customers!

DEVELOPER

Dued1

This pizza-loving developer has been part of the community since 2007. His masterpiece, Work at a Pizza Place, was the first game on Roblox to reach the landmark of one million favorites!

A TALE OF TWO RDCs

The Roblox Developers Conference sprung up on both sides of the Atlantic in 2017, with events in California and London, as well as livestreams that garnered over 200,000 views. We take a behind-the-scenes peek below.

SAN JOSE, CALIFORNIA

At the end of July 2017 in San Jose, California, a short journey away from Roblox HQ, a weekend full of fun awaited the developers who were lucky enough to receive one of the exclusive invites.

AN EDUCATION

A lot of the attendees were already among the most successful developers on Roblox, but there's always something new to learn. The various members of the Roblox team put on several more specific presentations, covering everything from Game Design 101 to Merchandising and Licensing.

WELCOME PARTY

The weekend began with some Friday evening entertainment, which included giant arcade games, a DJ, and an app-based icebreaker activity designed by the Roblox community to help devs meet new friends.

GAME JAM

To top off the weekend, RDC hosted the first of the Game Jam competitions, where attendees had just four hours to create a game, showcase, or build based on the theme "machines." The winners in the game category were zKevin, Phenite, Mah_Bucket, PressurizedSphere, and Iwishforpie1 and their creation FAXSTORY.

SHOWSTOPPER

After a night of fun and games, RDC began on Saturday, where David "Builderman" Baszucki and the rest of the Roblox team delivered presentations on the latest tech, using the platform as an education tool, and Roblox's domination of app store rankings.

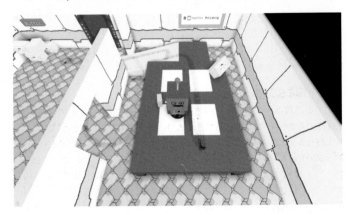

LONDON, ENGLAND

Mere weeks had passed before the Roblox team hopped across the pond and arrived at YouTube Space London for RDC Europe. The Global Dev community got a chance to meet in London for networking and to learn about new Roblox features.

CHAMPION

London's RDC had one thing that its predecessor didn't – the Roblox Tournament, which pitted five hand-selected competitors in battle across three games: Volt, Polyguns, and Ultimate Boxing. The winner was ROBLOX_Clothing, a bespoke tailor of avatar items, who just edged out MasterOfTheElements for the trophy.

VIRTUAL VISIT

Builderman couldn't make the trip to London, but he made sure he was still a part of it by delivering his segments via video call during the party. The London contingent then had the opportunity to sample talks and presentations on multiple areas of the Roblox platform.

JAM SESSION: TAKE 2

Visitors to London also had the opportunity to take part in the Game Jam. Having narrowly missed out on the Roblox Tournament prize, MasterOfTheElements landed first place in the game category for Ice, Wind, & Fire, created with his team of Jjwood1600, Zomebody, Arch_Mage, and Bluay.

INFLUENCERS

Following the Roblox team to England were YouTube stars and Robloxians DollasticDreams and MicroGuardian. The pair documented the whole weekend of the London conference, so check out their channels to see even more of the event.

INTRO TO STUDIO

Roblox Studio is an all-in-one tool that lets you build, code, and test your own games. It comes with every installation of Roblox, so you already have access to a world of creative possibilities. Here's a quick intro to help you get started in Studio. You'll be a game developer in no time!

GETTING STARTED
Open Roblox Studio by clicking the blue Roblox Studio icon. When you reach the landing screen, you'll see multiple templates you can try out. You can even create your own world from scratch by selecting the Baseplate template. Let's start with exploring the Pirate Island template.

EXPLORER
After opening the template, you can move the camera around by using the WASD keys and your mouse. On the right-hand side of the screen is the Explorer panel, which lists all the objects in your game. Click the name of the object to select it and make changes.

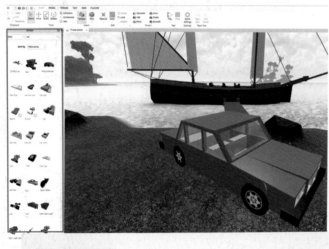

TOOLBOX
On the left-hand side of the screen is the Toolbox. Here, you can browse free models made by Roblox users like you. Double-click anything in the Toolbox to add it to your world.

PLAYTEST
The best way to get familiar with a template or a place you're creating is to jump right in! Click the Play button to drop your avatar into the world. Be sure to test any new additions to your world and see how they're looking. Click Stop when you're done.

TOOLS

Move, scale, rotate, and transform your objects by using the tools in the Model tab. Don't forget to playtest your game often as you make changes.

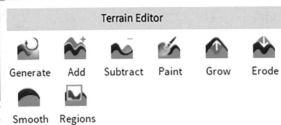

TERRAIN

Make changes to the terrain, such as adding lava or mountains, by using the Terrain tools. Here are a few of the most commonly used tools:

GENERATE

Randomly generates a new piece of terrain in your place. You can choose the size of the terrain and the mix of biomes that will be created.

ADD

Instantly creates new pieces of terrain out of nothing. It's best used for quickly adding large areas and features like rock arches. The opposite tool, Subtract, will delete pieces of terrain.

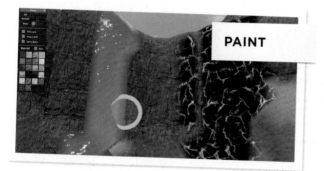

PAINT

Changes the type of terrain. Options include cement, sand, lava, water, and more. You can selectively paint areas to create icy mountain peaks or water that players can swim through.

GROW

Expands the selected terrain. This tool is great for creating gentle hills and more natural looking environments. The opposite tool, Erode, can be used for shrinking areas.

SMOOTH

Blends materials and terrain together so you don't have harsh lines between material types.

Now you'll be able to start creating and customizing your own world! But remember—this is just the tip of the Studio iceberg. You can add scripts to parts to make them more interactive, code new game mechanics, and combine places to create even larger universes. Anything you can imagine, you can make happen in Studio. To learn more, visit:

wiki.roblox.com

TOP 10 MOST-PLAYED GAMES ON ROBLOX

We all enjoy a little escapism and mystery now and then. Fortunately, the next games in our chart of most-played games fit both of these requirements. You'll need wit, guile, and the ability to look good in a jumpsuit if you're to master these action-survival classics!

4 PRISON LIFE

You don't want to spend your life in prison, do you? If you do find yourself behind bars, then assume the role of inmate, put on an orange jumpsuit, and plan your great escape. If you do want a life in prison, then you're the perfect candidate for the role of prison guard! With your nifty uniform, cuffs, and handgun, you'll have those crooks in line and back behind bars in no time!

3 MURDER MYSTERY 2

In Murder Mystery 2, you can experience the thrills, intrigue, and sheer panic of a PvP mystery battle. In each game, 12 players enter a map with one randomly allocated as the murderer and another as the sheriff. The remaining 10 players are innocents and have to survive for 180 seconds. Seems easy enough! You might even get to play a hero. If the sheriff is taken out, you can grab the dropped gun and take matters into your own hands!

THE MURDERER
As the murderer, you're armed with a knife. In the lobby, you can upgrade your murderous armory and purchase cool knives with a range of special powers and effects. The art of getting away with murder is to play it cool ... creep up and surprise your victims!

THE ROBLOX REDEMPTION

As a wrongly convicted inmate, your only alternative to a life behind bars is hatching an escape plan. Fortunately, there are lots of different ways to break free. You can steal a keycard and walk out the front door, or find a hammer and bash your way into the sewers, making a long, stinky crawl to freedom!

LIFE'S AN OPEN DOOR

Watch out for the automatic doors. As a guard, a mistimed entry or exit from the Guard Room can spark a riotous shootout. As an inmate, time it just right and you can dash through the door and out to your freedom!

CRIMINAL LIFE

Once you've done all the hard work getting out of prison, what's next? Life on the outside transforms you from an inmate into a hardened criminal with a new lease on life ... criminal life. You're now free to rescue your inmate buddies, shoot escaping inmates, or hunt down the prison guards that tormented you. You can even sneak back into the prison and cause a little criminal chaos!

DEVELOPER

Aesthetical

This snappily dressed prison governor and imaginative developer has been enjoying Roblox life since 2014. Prison Life was Aesthetical's breakout creation, and it has earned him three Bloxy Awards to date!

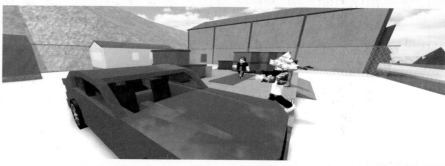

NEW SHERIFF IN TOWN

Each map is only big enough for one sheriff, and if you're given the badge of justice, then it's up to you to track down and deal with the murderer. You're the only player with a gun, so use it wisely, as the murderer is on the lookout for a gun-toting Robloxian to pick off next!

SECRET ROOMS!

Several Murder Mystery 2 maps have secret rooms that are the perfect place to hide if you're an innocent with a desire to survive for the whole 180 seconds. But the secret entrances aren't always so secret, and some murderers might be waiting in the shadows!

DEVELOPER

Nikilis

Murder Mystery 2 is a direct sequel to Nikilis's Murder Mystery which was one of the first games of its type. The original game pioneered the much-loved murder mystery genre on Roblox.

5TH ANNUAL BLOXY AWARDS HIGHLIGHTS

The Bloxy Awards applaud everything connected to Roblox, and beyond the games there is an ever-growing supportive and passionate community. From coders and builders to artists and social media stars, the whole Robloxian society receives honors at the ceremony. Here are the highlights of the celebrated community members that are the glue between the building blocks of Roblox.

BEST LOBBY

Murder Mystery 2
There's nothing like a relaxing lobby to hang out in and wait for the next round of your favorite Roblox experience, and the best of the best at the 5th Annual Awards went to Murder Mystery 2 by Nikilis.

FAVORITE SHOWCASE

Apartment 23
Along with games, Roblox also has some beautifully crafted places to visit. And this year's Showcase award went to the imaginative and masterful showcase, Apartment 23 by Joseph155.

FAVORITE LIVE STREAMER

berezaa
Where would Roblox be without its gamers? This year's live streamer award went to an old favorite, with gamer, developer, and community star berezaa, famous for Epic Mining and Azure Mines, picking up the award.

BEST VIDEO CHANNEL

EthanGamerTV
After being overlooked at two previous Bloxy awards, the 11-year-old super-gamer and YouTube sensation EthanGamer found success at the 5th Annual Bloxys, picking up the award for best video channel!

BEST NEW DEV TEAM

Novaly Studios

Roblox is growing every year and continues to power imagination for veterans and newcomers alike. The award for New Dev Team went to Novaly Studios, creators of the shooter Wild Revolvers.

BEST GUI

Robloxian Highschool

When you're playing games, you sometimes look past the graphical user interface and just sit back and play, but some can be innovative and cleverly styled, like this year's winner of Best GUI, Robloxian Highschool!

MORE AWARDS

Best Showcase Render
Zyleth & FramedChrisRBLX

Best Original Character
asimo3089

Best Comedic Video
Top 5 Jailbreak Fails

Best Action Video
STREET FIGHT

Best Music Video
ROBLOX SONG "Create"

Best GIF
Roblox Survivor

Best Original Music Score
Heroes of Robloxia

Best Game Trailer
Vehicle Simulator

Best Custom Items
Welcome to Bloxburg

Best Tweet
MeepCity

Best Game Logo
Epic Minigames

Best Twitter Channel
ItsFunneh

Best Avatar Render
IDontHaveAUse

Best Roblox Dev Toy
asimo3089

Most Improved
Vehicle Simulator

Most Social
Water Park

Community Excellence
Wild Revolvers

Technical Achievement
MeepCity

Best New Breakout Game
Adopt Me

Favorite Map
Flee the Facility

BEST FAN ART

IDontHaveAUse

Robloxia is full of creative individuals all bringing their skills to the community and millions of games. This year's standout artist was IDontHaveAUse for his artwork based on Badimo's Jailbreak.

BEST CLOTHING COMPANY

Boho Salon

This fashionista award for excellence in clothing design went to Lalakiela and her fashion group Boho Salon, which has nearly one million members!

EXCELLENCE IN ANIMATION

Robot 64

As the capabilities of Roblox Studio evolve, so do the talents of the animators that create exciting experiences. This year's award for excellence in animation went to Robot 64 by zKevin.

GAMES YOU MAY HAVE MISSED

The next stops on our tour of Roblox's hidden gems involve exploration and discovery with a splash of heroism. Some places on Roblox are beautiful and mesmerizing in their aesthetic, while others offer more comical entertainment. Here are some more experiences you may have missed on your gaming adventures.

LIFE OF AN OTAKU

This outstanding experience takes you beyond the bloxy aesthetic into an ultra-realistic world. An "otaku" is a person obsessed with computers and pop culture, to the detriment of a social life. The showcase uses this idea to create an interactive experience that draws the player into a solitary life.

SHOWCASE AND TELL
As with most showcases on Roblox, the world is sculpted with a masterful artistic touch. What takes this hidden gem to another level is the variety of interactions the player can have with the world.

EXPLORE SOME MORE
The home alone is a captivating experience, with many rooms and details to discover, but beyond the house is an equally engaging world to explore, with a courtyard, shrine, and more to discover.

Developer
YasuYoshida

The awesomely talented YasuYoshida is still adding and crafting more aspects to his elegant showcase, and hopes to add even more moments of wonder for players to discover.

HEROES OF ROBLOXIA

There comes a time in every gamer's life when herodom beckons, when you just have to don a mask and battle the forces of evil. Heroes of Robloxia lets you do just that. At the start of the game, you can choose from one of four superheroes before completing missions to defeat your arch-nemesis Darkmatter and foil his nefarious plans for world domination!

MISSION TIME

This hero caper is full of action-packed missions that you can play alone or with others. Each one pits you against a different supervillain and their goons, and involves lots of fighting, puzzles, and platforming.

PLAYER BATTLE

If you've completed the missions, or are just in the mood for gladiatorial fun, you can also compete in the player vs. player arena, where superheroes fight it out to be crowned arena champion by knocking out and defeating other gamers.

Select Your Power

Telekinesis	Speed	Strength	Electricity
Kinetic	Overdrive	Captain Roblox	Tessla

TIP... The four heroes offer different ways to play the game. Don't worry if you're struggling on a level because you can switch to certain heroes during each of the missions, enabling the use of different powers to complete puzzles.

Developer
Team Super

Heroes of Robloxia's origin story goes back to 2017 and was scripted by Team Super, a game-creation studio owned by developer InsanelyLuke, and released during Roblox's Heroes event.

WHOBLOXEDWHO'S FAVORITE GAMES!

WhoBloxedWho? We don't know, but what we do know is this enigmatic dev has been playing on Roblox since 2009. He's one of the brains behind Team Rudimentality and their hit game Strobe 2. So, we've tracked him down to question him about his favorite Roblox games, and why he loves them.

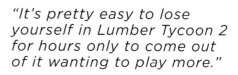

"It's pretty easy to lose yourself in Lumber Tycoon 2 for hours only to come out of it wanting to play more."

LUMBER TYCOON 2

First up on WhoBloxedWho's list of all-time favorite Roblox games is Lumber Tycoon 2. For WhoBloxedWho, there's nothing more relaxing than this tranquil gaming experience by Defaultio, and who doesn't like a little soothing lumberjacking and forestry exploration?

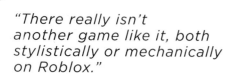

"There really isn't another game like it, both stylistically or mechanically on Roblox."

CUBE CAVERN

The next bloxy great on WhoBloxedWho's list of awesome Roblox games is Cube Cavern by zKevin. This dungeon-based adventure makes WhoBloxedWho appreciate what's truly possible on Roblox with its unique styling and absorbing gameplay.

3

> *"The community around the game is great."*

TALES FROM THE VALLEY

This epic adventure features magic, power, and dozens of inventive quests! WhoBloxedWho's next all-time favorite game is Arch_Mage's fantasy adventure, Tales from the Valley, which was released in 2016. He loves the beautiful world, the mystery, and the unique playing experience that evolves each time you start a new game.

4

> *"Its platforming mechanics and introspective plot makes for a really wholesome experience."*

RAMONA

Number four on WhoBloxedWho's top games is a rarity on Roblox – a single-player game! Ramona by Captain_Arr's Party is a mysterious 3D platformer with a clever plot and retro-inspired aesthetic. It has multiple endings too, meaning you'll need to play multiple times to see all sides of the story. Over a million fans have played the game since its release.

> *"A timeless classic that has been around since I first started playing Roblox."*

5

ARMORED PATROL

The final piece to the enigmatic WhoBloxedWho's puzzle of favorite games is Wingman8's battle classic Armored Patrol. WhoBloxedWho loves teaming up with his friends for an epic all-terrain, missile-fuelled battle-fest, and has played it since he joined Roblox!

FAMOUS HATS THROUGH THE AGES

Hats have become a phenomenon on Roblox as the go-to statement piece to set players apart from the crowd, ranging from extravagant fedoras to majestic crowns. Take a look at some of the headwear masterpieces, all created exclusively by the Roblox team, that have taken the Catalog by storm over the years.

DOMINO CROWN
2007
An ostentatious golden crown styled after a domino, which was awarded to winners of the Domino Rally Building Contest in 2007. It may look slightly silly, but it's highly sought after by collectors.

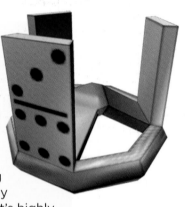

WANWOOD ANTLERS
2007
A perfect symbiosis between flora and fauna, these staggering antlers have been carved from the finest woods. No animals were harmed in the making of this adornment.

THE ICE CROWN
2008
Formerly belonging to the last empress of Charn, this frosty crown is a hot commodity in the Catalog. Getting your (gloved) hands on this piece will make you super-cool.

VALKYRIE HELM
2008
This headpiece, inspired by minor gods of Norse mythology, is the perfect addition to any mythical outfit. It's based on the Valkyries, the Norse enforcers of justice.

DOMINUS EMPYREUS
2010

This is one of the most famous and desired garments on Roblox. Its simple white cowl and feathered ornamentation were an instant hit, and spawned a whole Dominus series.

RED GRIND
2010

Created by Robloxia's foremost skating brand,):, this cap is clean and simple. However, its relative scarcity has skyrocketed the item's price to well over 200,000 Robux!

RAINBOW SHAGGY
2011

Tidy hair is overrated, and picking a single hair color is so boring. This next item has you covered on both fronts, with a disheveled cut and a vast spectrum of hues.

RED SPARKLE TIME FEDORA
2012

Made famous by star developer Cindering, this simple red fedora has been embellished with the Sparkle Time treatment, adding a shiny polygonistic texture to an old classic.

LORD OF THE FEDERATION
2012

A galactic crown embellished with golden moons and stars grants the wearer dominion over the cosmos and the reunited federation. There are only ten in circulation!

GLORIOUS PINK PARTY QUEEN
2015

Inspired by masquerade parties of Robloxia and Venezia alike, this item combines flowing black locks with a bright pink fox mask to create a formidable statement piece.

VOIDWRATH
2016

Dress to dismay with this headpiece, a manifestation of a malevolent being that has conquered all realms of Earth and Robloxia, complete with hovering cosmic sigils.

SPARKLE TIME VALKYRIE
2017

Blessed by the leader of the Valkyries herself, the goddess Freya, this kaleidoscopic rework of the classic Valkyrie headdress adds an extra dimension to an already amazing item.

DEVELOPER LESSONS: BUILDING

If you've designed your game, you should be ready to get your hands dirty and start the long, arduous task of building! Luckily for you, busy builder Beeism is here to pass on words of wisdom regarding Roblox Studio and building cool game worlds.

PLAN AND TEST

"The first step to making a great map is to have a solid plan with a lot of wiggle room," says Beeism. Start with a sketch on paper first. Once you have a good, flexible plan, rough it out in Roblox Studio as quickly as possible using simple shapes and colors. Don't add details like buildings or plants yet. The sooner you have the general shape of your map, the sooner you can test it out and make changes without re-doing a lot of work.

DESIGN THE TERRAIN

Once you're satisfied with the basic shape of the map, add terrain. Use the Add, Grow, and Smooth terrain tools to create a world around your basic shapes. Make sure you have plenty of space for things you have planned, like houses, dungeon entrances, and quest areas. At this stage, the terrain should be close to final, but it doesn't have to be perfect.

WORK LARGE TO SMALL

Now that you've established the shape of your terrain, start adding in large models such as houses and buildings. These could be from the Roblox Toolbox or models that you made. Consider how each object fits into your game. Maybe it needs to be easy to reach with a visible road leading to it, or maybe it's a secret and needs to be hidden! In Beeism's build, every house is special. "I tried to make sure each house had its own perk, whether it was a view of the ocean, a higher position on the mountain, or close to the water."

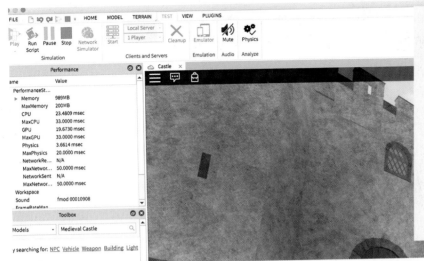

OPTIMIZE YOUR GAME

The more you add to your world, the harder computers have to work to run it. Nobody likes a laggy game. Make your game perform better by using low poly models, removing terrain nobody will see, and getting rid of unnecessary features. Moving objects also take up more memory than those that don't. Beeism has some advice on how to make your game run better: "If you have to use meshes, reuse and repurpose them whenever possible."

KEEP TESTING

At every stage of your game, keep playtesting. Check to see that there aren't any areas where players can get stuck or fall into the abyss. Get other people to play your game as well. Watch to see if they know where they are going and ask them what they think can be improved. Make sure your game still runs well, and remove small details if necessary. And don't just test on your computer, ask your friends to help you test on their phones, tablets, Xbox One, and computers.

POLISH YOUR MAP

After all of the large details—like buildings—have been finalized, it's time to start adding the finishing touches. "This is when you add the things that make it come to life," says Beeism. First, add medium-sized models, like trees, and place any NPCs or enemies. Then, start adding small decorative items such as plants, hidden Easter eggs, or signs. Keep in mind that too many little things will slow down your game.

ROBLOX MERCH

Are you a Roblox super-fan? Have you consumed an eclectic mix of amazing items, gear, and bespoke avatar packages? Well, here's more great news! Your love of Roblox is no longer confined to the digital realm! Roblox has released its awesomeness into the real world with items you can wear, collect, and play with!

ROBLOX STYLE

Roblox has created their own line of awesome T-shirts! You can now dress from neck to waist in Roblox style, so you can show off your love of the Imagination Platform wherever you go!

Let your Roblox colors run with this two-tone tee featuring the Roblox icon.

You can never have too much Roblox, nor can you have too many Roblox logos!

Builderman explored the meta side of fashion with this schematic tee.

Ezebel: The Pirate Queen is front and foremost on this character combo.

This simple, subtle icon T-shirt is an understated gem.

Celebrate the absurdity of Mr. Robot with this cool character tee.

ROBLOXAPEDIAS

To grow your all-encompassing knowledge of the Imagination Platform, Roblox has written some wise words, gathered a collection of cool renders, and weaved them into two awesome books.

CHARACTER ENCYCLOPEDIA

For the complete Who's Who of Roblox, this epic encyclopedia is packed with everything you need to know about all your favorite characters that make the world of Roblox so ... characterful.

TOP ADVENTURE GAMES

Want to know all there is to know about the coolest adventure games on Roblox? This anthology of awesome adventure games is all you need! It also has lots of cool pictures!

THE TOYBLOX

With such a breadth of talent on the platform, you can imagine it is tough to choose which characters to immortalize as toys. Luckily, Roblox was up to the challenge and has released wave after wave of amazing figures.

COLLECTOR'S TOOL BOX
Take your awesome Roblox figures wherever you go with this handy carry case.

GAME PACKS
Reenact scenes from your favorite Roblox experiences with packs based on popular games.

PLAYSETS
These giant sets include characters from across Robloxia, as well as lots of accessories.

VEHICLES
Get your action figures on the road with these speedy vehicle sets.

THINKING INSIDE THE BLOX?
If you like a surprise, then the Mystery Figure line is for you. On the outside, the Roblox boxes look pretty much the same, but on the inside of these cryptic crates is a range of characters to collect! Can you find them all?

TOP 10 MOST-PLAYED GAMES ON ROBLOX

We have reached the zenith of our epic, top-ten most-played Roblox games! You might've already guessed the last two games occupying the top spots ... they're kind of a big deal. Hopefully you still have your orange jumpsuit available and are ready for a little role-play.

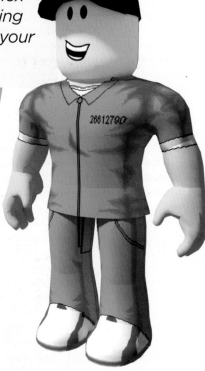

2 JAILBREAK

This much-awarded classic has risen to the top of the prison-escape genre and expanded beyond the prison walls. Players start with a simple choice between police or prisoner roles. Prisoners start in jail, focused on escape, whereas the police have the job of keeping them behind bars. But don't be fooled into thinking this game is just about the jail. There's a big wide world out there to explore ... you just need an escape plan!

1 MEEPCITY

Welcome to the wonderful world of MeepCity. This hugely popular social hangout game tops our chart, and with good reason – it's the first game to reach over a billion visits. MeepCity is an open-world experience where players can earn money, play minigames, socialize with friends, and find a place to call home. Players can also adopt a pet called a Meep and dress it up with lots of cool gear!

MEEP AND ME

Meeps are in-game pets and can be bought from the pet shop along with a wide array of cool Meep items and clothes. Once you've chosen your Meep, you get to name it and choose its color. Your Meep will now float and follow you wherever you go! You can even buy it toys and furniture.

KEYCARDS ARE KEY

There are lots of ways to escape in Jailbreak, from climbing the fence and exploding a wall, to stealing a guard's keycard. To get your hands on a valuable keycard, creep behind a guard and perform the pickpocket action! Keycards also come in handy during bank heists, gaining you easy access to the bank and its vaults.

A CRIMINAL WORLD

Where Jailbreak differs from other games in the genre is its expansive world. It's huge and has many places to explore, hide, and rob! Head to the criminal base to equip your ex-con with everything you need, then explore the map to continue your career of crime!

DEVELOPER

Badimo

This game-creation studio was formed by the outrageously talented badcc and asimo3089. To date, Jailbreak is Badimo's only endeavor, and it's done pretty well since release, receiving over a billion visits.

HEIST HEAVEN

In the large world map, there are lots of criminal activities an ex-con can indulge in, from robbing stores to performing an epic bank heist! There are also weapons to find, and when you've stolen a little cash you can spend it on a flashy car to improve your chances of a getaway. But watch out for the cops - they roam the map looking to collect the bounty on your head.

GAMES CITY

MeepCity isn't just about chilling out with friends and decorating your estate—there are also lots of cool games to play including the marble-madness-style obby Star Ball and the hugely addictive MeepCity Racing.

COINS FOR CASH

The in-game currency in MeepCity is coins. You earn coins by spending time in the game, but you can increase your bank balance by fishing at the city ponds, then selling your catch of the day at the pet shop. You can also earn extra coins as you play the many MeepCity minigames!

DEVELOPER

Alexnewtron

This record-breaking developer has been concocting awesome Roblox experiences since 2007 and his portfolio includes DODGEBALL! and Club DJ, as well as the epically popular MeepCity.

65

RECAP QUIZ

If you've reached this point, then you should know the world of Roblox inside-out. To make sure you've been paying attention, we've put together a quick test to see how much you can remember. See how many you can answer, then try to find the answers throughout the book for any that are too tricky.

EASY

Let's start with some simple questions to warm up. Maybe you even knew these before you read the book?

What is the name of David Baszucki's original avatar?

☐ Fireman   ☐ Builderman   ☐ Policeman

What's the name of the current avatar model?

☐ R6   ☐ R15   ☐ R29

Which type of item can only be created by the Roblox team?

☐ Gear   ☐ Accessories   ☐ Hats

Which of these characters is not a superhero in Heroes of Robloxia?

☐ Tessla   ☐ Mr. Robot   ☐ Captain Roblox

What is the name of the program used to create places and games for Roblox?

☐ Roblox Workshop   ☐ Roblox Studio   ☐ Roblox Forge

Which game was the first on Roblox to reach 1 billion visits?

☐ Neverland Lagoon   ☐ Jailbreak   ☐ MeepCity

MEDIUM

These questions are a little bit trickier, but shouldn't be too difficult for a super fan like you!

Which developer created Lumber Tycoon 2?

☐ Defaultio ☐ Maelstronomer ☐ Dizzypurple

RDC was held in two locations in 2017 – which countries were they?

☐ Canada & USA ☐ USA & England ☐ England & Canada

One of the hottest items in the Catalog is a mix of an animal and a fruit – which combo is correct?

☐ Avocado & Spider ☐ Banana & Monkey ☐ Watermelon & Shark

What was the name of the first limited edition item available in the Catalog?

☐ Collector's Item ☐ Rare Item ☐ Limited Edition Item

HARD

Okay, now you might need to flip back through the book to find some answers.

Where was Roblox's first office?

☐ Menlo Park ☐ Central Park ☐ Asbury Park

Which Roblox event usually occurs around late March/early April each year?

☐ The Bloxys ☐ Egg Hunt ☐ Summer Games

Which developer won the Lifetime Achievement Award at the 5th Annual Bloxys?

☐ Shedletsky ☐ Merely ☐ Stickmasterluke

Which item was awarded to winners of the Domino Rally Building Contest?

☐ Domino Dress ☐ Domino Crown ☐ Domino Sword

Which game is RickyTheFishy's favorite?

☐ Moon Tycoon ☐ Clone Tycoon 2 ☐ Lumber Tycoon 2

SEE YOU ON ROBLOX!

I hope you enjoyed this journey into the world of Roblox. I feel honored to be part of a community whose boundless imagination has brought to life some of the most creative games and experiences I have ever seen.

At Roblox, we are driven to create the largest entertainment platform for play where there are countless opportunities to imagine, learn, and build with hundreds of millions of people all over the world. As I sit here reading through this book, I am proud of our evolution and what we have been able to accomplish over the years. Roblox will continue to become even more social and more immersive, and we will provide creators with better tools to build and share quality experiences in ways never thought possible.

Whether you are new to Roblox, or an aspiring developer creating the next big hit, we appreciate your support and passion. I look forward to all the exciting things that your imagination will bring to Roblox.

Sincerely,
David Baszucki, a.k.a. Builderman

A GUIDE TO SOCIALIZING ONLINE WITH ROBLOX

YOUNGER FANS' GUIDE TO ROBLOX

Spending time online is great fun! Roblox might be your first experience of digital socializing, so here are a few simple rules to help you stay safe and keep the internet a great place to spend time.

- *Never give out your real name – don't use it as your username.*
- *Never give out any of your personal details.*
- *Never tell anybody which school you go to or how old you are.*
- *Never tell anybody your password except a parent or guardian.*
- *Always tell a parent or guardian if something is worrying you.*

PARENTS' GUIDE TO ROBLOX

Roblox has security and privacy settings that enable you to monitor and limit your child's access to the social features on Roblox, or turn them off completely. You can also limit the range of games your child can access, view their activity histories, and report inappropriate activity on the site. Instructions for how to use these safety features are listed below.

NAVIGATING ROBLOX'S SAFETY FEATURES

*To restrict your child from playing, chatting, and messaging with others on Roblox, log into your child's account and click on the **gear icon** in the upper right-hand corner of the site and select **Settings**. From here you can access the **Security** and **Privacy** menus:*

- *Users register for Roblox with their date of birth. It's important for children to enter the correct date because Roblox has default security and privacy settings that vary based on a player's age. This can be checked and changed in **Settings**.*

- *To review and restrict your child's social settings, go to **Settings** and select **Privacy**. Review the options under **Contact Settings** and **Other Settings**. Select **No one** or **Everyone**. Note: players age 13 and older have additional options.*

- *To control the safety features that are implemented on your child's account, you'll need to set up a 4-digit PIN. This will lock all of the settings, only enabling changes once the PIN is entered. To enable an Account PIN, go to the **Settings** page, select **Security**, and turn **Account PIN** to **ON**.*

To help monitor your child's account, you can view the history for certain activities:

- *To view your child's private message history, choose **Messages** from the menu bar down the left-hand side of the main screen. If the menu bar isn't visible, click on the **LIST** icon in the left-hand corner.*

- *To view your child's chat history with other players, open the **Chat & Party** window, located in the bottom-right of the page. Once this window is opened, you can click on any of the listed users to open a window with the chat history for that particular account.*

- *To view your child's online friends and followers, choose **Friends** from the menu bar down the left-hand side of the main screen.*

- *To view your child's creations, such as games, items, trades, and sounds, choose **Develop** from the tabs along the top of the main screen.*

- *To view any virtual items purchased and any trade history, choose **Trade** from the menu bar down the left-hand side of the main screen, then go to **My Transactions**.*

While the imagery on Roblox has a largely blocky, digitized look, parents should be aware that some of the user-generated games may include themes or imagery that may be too intense for young or sensitive players:

- *You can limit your child's account to display only a restricted list of available games to play. Go to **Settings**, select **Security**, and turn on **Account Restrictions**.*

Roblox players of all ages have their posts and chats filtered to prevent personal information from being shared, but no filter is foolproof. Roblox asks users and parents to report any inappropriate activity. Check your child's account and look to see if they have friends they do not know, and talk to your child about what to report (including bullying, inappropriate behavior or messages, scams, and other game violations):

- *To report concerning behavior on Roblox, players and parents can use the **Report Abuse** links located on game, group, and user pages and in the **Report** tab of every game menu.*

- *To block another player during a game session, find the user on the leaderboard/player list at the upper-right of the game screen. (If the leaderboard/player list isn't there, open it by clicking on your username in the upper-right corner.) From here, click on the player you wish to block and select **Block User**.*

For further information and help, Roblox has created a parents' guide to the website which can be accessed at https://corp.roblox.com/parents